zendoodle coloring
COLOR-by-NUMBER

Sea Life

zendoodle coloring
COLOR-by-NUMBER

Sea Life
Underwater Worlds to Color and Display

illustrations by
Jeanette Wummel

ST. MARTIN'S GRIFFIN
NEW YORK

www.stmartins.com

ISBN 978-1-250-14074-6 (trade paperback)

Our books may be purchased in bulk for promotional, educational, or business use.
Please contact your local bookseller or the Macmillan Corporate and Premium
Sales Department at 1-800-221-7945, extension 5442, or by e-mail
at MacmillanSpecialMarkets@macmillan.com.

First Edition: July 2017

10 9 8 7 6 5 4 3 2

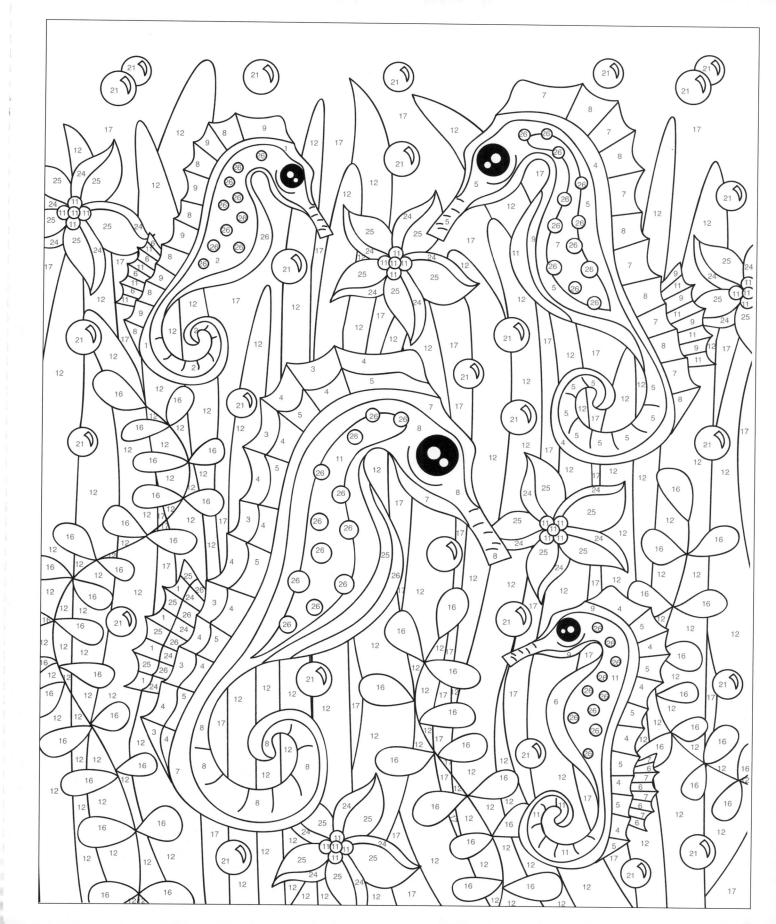

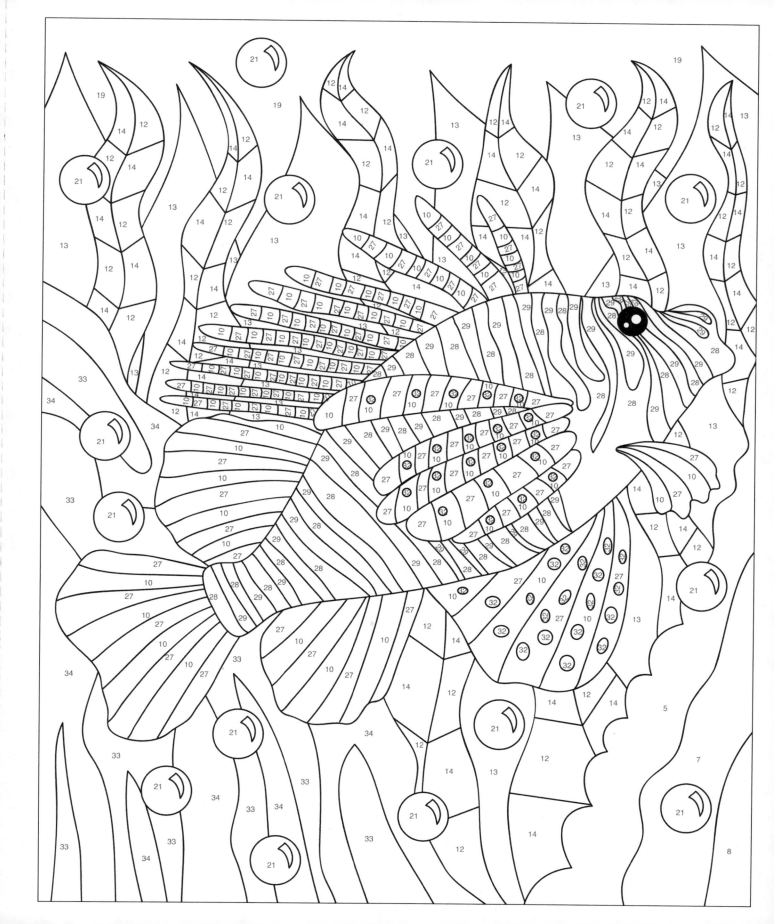

Other great books in the series

zendoodle
color-by-number series

Stained Glass

Spring Awakening

Playful Pets

Other great books in the

zendoodle coloring series

Celestial Wonders

Loving Expressions

Baby Animals

Birds and Butterflies

Magical Mermaid Kitties

Playful Puppies

Hopeful Inspirations

and many more!